Balloons

Macdonald

About Macdonald Starters

Macdonald Starters are vocabulary controlled information books for young children. More than ninety per cent of the words in the text will be in the reading vocabulary of the vast majority of young readers. Word and sentence length have also been carefully controlled.

Key new words associated with the topic of each book are repeated with picture explanations in the Starters dictionary at the end. The dictionary can also be used as an index for teaching children to look things up.

Teachers and experts have been consulted on the content and accuracy of the books.

A MACDONALD BOOK

© Macdonald & Co (Publishers) Ltd 1973

First published in
Great Britain in 1973

This edition first published in
Great Britain in 1986

British Library Cataloguing in Publication Data
Vaughan, Jennifer
Balloons. – (Starters)
    1. Readers – 1950 –
    I. Title   II. Mousdale, John
    428.6   PE1119

    ISBN 0-356-04334-7
    ISBN 0-356-11497-X Pbk

Printed and bound in Great Britain by
Purnell & Sons (Book Production) Ltd,
Paulton, Bristol

Published by Macdonald & Co (Publishers) Ltd
Maxwell House
74 Worship Street
London EC2A 2EN

Members of BPCC plc

Illustrator: John Mousdale

We are having a party.
Daddy is blowing up the balloons.

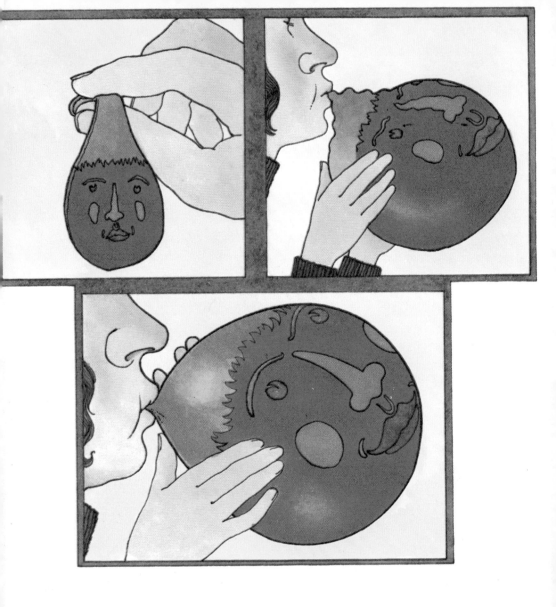

The balloon gets bigger and bigger.
The face on it gets bigger too.

2

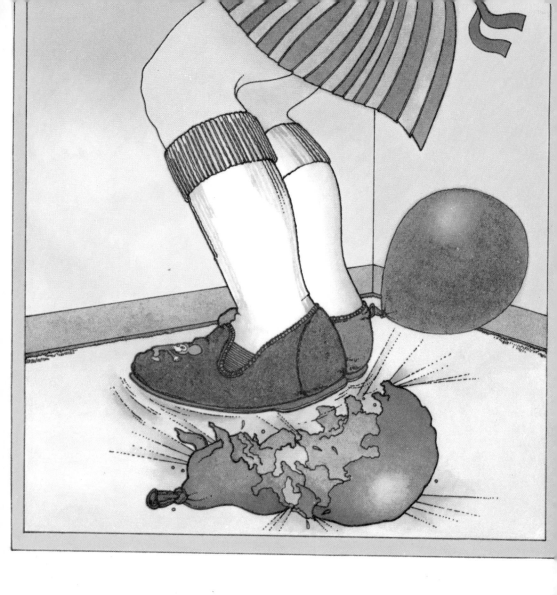

I am jumping on this balloon.
It bursts.

I blew this balloon up.
Then I let it go.
It flew round the room.

4

It is a windy day.
My balloon has blown away.

I bought a balloon at a fair.
It is filled with hydrogen gas.
It can go high in the air.

6

Some people race hydrogen balloons.
They see whose balloon
goes the furthest.

7

This large hydrogen balloon
goes high into the air.
It carries lots of equipment.

8

The equipment with the balloon
sends signals to the earth.
Scientists learn about the weather
from the signals.

Long ago people used balloons to fly.
They rode in a basket.
The basket hung below the balloon.
10

Some people like to race in balloons.
The balloons are like
balloons long ago.

These soldiers used a balloon.
The men in the basket looked out
for enemies.

12

Sometimes letters were sent
by balloon.
They were sent to places
where there were no roads.

Enemies were all round this city.
The people inside
sent pigeons out by balloon.
14

message

The pigeons landed beyond the enemy.
People fixed messages to their legs.
The pigeons carried these
back to the city.

15

This is an airship.
It is like a long balloon.
It has engines.
16

People travelled in airships.
The cabin looked like this inside.

17

Airships were dangerous.
They caught fire easily.
So people stopped using them.

18

These are barrage balloons.
People used them in war time.
Bombers could not fly among them
and drop bombs.

19

This was the first balloon
to carry people.
It was filled with hot air.
This made it fly.

20

People can make small hot air
balloons.
These men have made two.
The balloons may fly a long way.

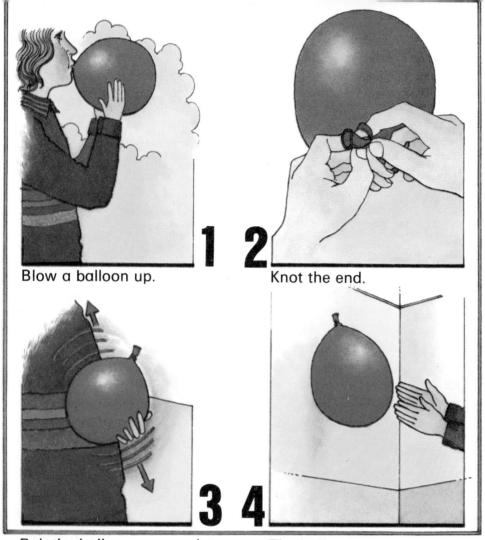

1 Blow a balloon up.

2 Knot the end.

3 Rub the balloon on your jersey.

4 The balloon should stick to the wall or the ceiling.

See for yourself
Try this trick with a balloon.

22

Starter's **Balloons** words

party
(page 1)

burst
(page 3)

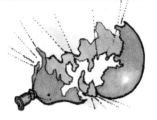

blowing
(page 1)

flew
(page 4)

balloons
(page 1)

hydrogen
balloon
(page 6)

face
(page 2)

balloon
race
(page 7)

jump
(page 3)

equipment
(page 8)

23

earth
(page 9)

scientist
(page 9)

fly
(page 10)

basket
(page 10)

soldiers
(page 12)

look out
(page 12)

letters
(page 13)

city
(page 14)

pigeon
(page 14)

message
(page 15)

airship
(page 16)

engine
(page 16)

cabin
(page 17)

fire
(page 18)

barrage balloon
(page 19)
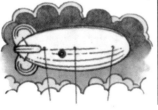

bomber
(page 19)
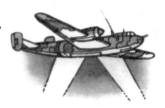

bomb
(page 19)

hot air balloon
(page 20)

jersey
(page 22)

wall
(page 22)

25